**English
Language
Teacher
Development
Series**

Classroom Research for Language Teachers

TIM STEWART

*Second
Edition*

Thomas S. C. Farrell, *Series Editor*

bookstore.tesol.org

TESOL International Association
1925 Ballenger Avenue, Ste. 550
Alexandria, VA 22314 USA
www.tesol.org

Managing Editor: Tomiko Breland
Copy Editor: Elizabeth Adler
Cover and Interior Design: Kathleen Dyson
Head of Education & Events: Sarah Sahr

Recommended citation:
Stewart, T. (2023). *Classroom research for language teachers* (2nd ed.). TESOL International Association.

ISBN 978-1-953745-32-3
ISBN (ebook) 978-1-953745-33-0
Library of Congress Control Number 2023938958

Contents

In memory of my parents, who set me on my path.

Series Editor's Preface

The English Language Teacher Development (ELTD) series consists of a set of short resource books for English language teachers that are written in a jargon-free and accessible manner for all types of teachers of English, including experienced and novice teachers. The ELTD series is designed to offer teachers a theory-to-practice approach to English language teaching, and each book offers a wide variety of practical teaching approaches and methods for the topic at hand. Each book also offers opportunities for teachers to interact with the materials presented. The books can be used in preservice settings or in-service courses and by individuals looking for ways to refresh their practice.

Tim Stewart's second edition of *Classroom Research for Language Teachers* further explores different approaches to conducting classroom research in the English language classroom. This updated and comprehensive overview of how to approach classroom research is an easy-to-follow guide that language teachers will find very practical for their own contexts. Topics covered include getting started with research, collecting data, analyzing and interpreting data, publishing findings, and continuing with classroom research beyond one project. In addition, there are new examples of teacher research and more resources for language teachers wishing to conduct their own research. *Classroom Research for Language Teachers, Second Edition,* is a valuable addition to the literature in our profession.

I am very grateful to the authors of the ELTD series for sharing their knowledge and expertise with other English language teaching professionals to make these short books affordable for all language teachers throughout the world. It is truly an honor for me to work again with each of these authors for the advancement of English language teaching.

Thomas S. C. Farrell

CHAPTER 1

Teachers and Research

As an English language teacher, what is your relationship with research? Do you read it, ignore it, or simply dismiss it? Would you do it? Many readers will answer *no* to this last question. The purpose of this book is to get you to say *yes*, or at the very least, *maybe*. I believe that all teachers should engage in classroom research from time to time. This book is a guide for novice teacher-researchers.

This chapter will seek answers to these questions:

- Why should English language teachers conduct classroom research?

- What will English language teachers learn from this book?

Mind the Gap

Reflecting on her time hosting university researchers in her classroom for an extended period, Schecter (1997) explained that while conducting their study, the researchers never bothered to ask her what she thought, nor did they return later to explain their results. In short, a lot of research is being done *on* teachers and students rather than *with* or *by* teachers and students (Stewart, 2006a). A main effect of this continuing situation is that "there is a great deal of distrust of theory among English language teachers. They tend to see it as remote from their actual experience, an attempt to mystify common-sense practices by unnecessary abstraction" (Widdowson, 2003, p. 1). Echoing Widdowson, Kiely (2014) states, "If teachers feel researchers do not understand their task in classroom teaching, they are unlikely to be persuaded to innovate or experiment" (p. 443) based on published research findings. The situation was highlighted in the 100th anniversary issue of the influential *Modern Language Journal* by the editor as the "often-times noxious research versus teaching dichotomy" (Byrnes, 2016, p. 7).

Over 40 years ago, Michael Long stressed the significance of practitioners researching their own practice. Long (1984) observed that early classroom research studies revealed "what actually goes on in [English as a second language] classrooms, as opposed to what is believed to go on, and as distinct from what writers on [teaching English as a second language] methods tell us ought to go on" (p. 422). A decade later, Donald Freeman (1996) lamented: "For too long teaching has been treated as something which certain people do and others research....Thus, teachers are constantly having what they know defined for them by others" (p. 106). This attitude reveals the schism within English language teaching (ELT) that still exists based upon the common hierarchy of credibility in the field (Sato & Loewen, 2019); researchers research and publish, teachers teach, and students study. Unfortunately, this hierarchy often results in the production of publications in the field that practitioners see as "'out of touch' with the day-to-day realities [of teachers]" (Montgomery & Smith, 2015, p. 100). The gap is real. The question is how to narrow it.

 REFLECTIVE BREAK

Think of a published book or article that you found useful in your practice. Why do you think you were able to find value in it?

A Passion for Teaching

Classroom teaching is demanding work. There is just so much to know and learn. Secretly, you might feel unsure about your teaching ability in the first few years while you operate in survival mode. With experience, you develop a toolkit of techniques and tasks to draw from. Your confidence will surely increase, and you will begin to notice more about your teaching and your students.

At the point where you can easily manage the basics of classroom practice, your level of anxiety will decrease. It is at this learning plateau that some teachers begin to coast a bit. Sooner or later, most teachers will stop making progress in their professional development. At this point, their satisfaction with their knowledge about the practice of teaching typically decreases. The actively reflective teacher will realize once again that there is much more to learn to become a better classroom teacher. When you begin to feel like your teaching practice is stagnating, how can you renew it and regain satisfaction in the classroom?

Once you move beyond the novice teacher's survival mode and gain control over the basics of teaching practice, you create space within your professional practice that allows you to begin to see new things about your teaching, your students, and the language content. Increased control raises your confidence to do certain tasks without excessive planning and anxiety over implementation. In addition, this confidence opens up the space needed for inquiry. You will begin to wonder, for example, why certain lessons did or did not go well or why some students have trouble with a particular aspect of grammar. The source of such questions is your instinct to learn more about your practice.

Generally, teachers simply want to focus on improving their teaching. Over time, however, puzzling aspects of teaching and learning accumulate. These unresolved issues present you with a choice. You can push these nagging questions aside and focus on doing your best at your current level of knowledge, or you can decide to dig deeper into your passion for teaching through classroom research.

Teaching in the 21st Century

Besides a natural curiosity fuelled by a love of teaching, there are other pressing reasons why teachers should engage in classroom research. The climate in the field of English language education has changed. Foreign language teachers today generally enter the field with a higher level of expertise than previously expected. Many institutions seek candidates with graduate degrees. In addition, organizations such as TESOL International Association are professionalizing the field as never before. If language teachers wish to be treated like professionals in other fields, then they must engage in a broader array of professional activity. For those who wish to make ELT a career, classroom research opens the door to many valuable professional practices and work opportunities.

Despite there being many reasons for teachers to engage in research, some readers will doubt their ability to do classroom research. Perhaps they think research is something only college professors do. However, the current reality is that to better understand the complex processes of teaching and learning, the English language education field needs more classroom teachers to do classroom research (Stewart, 2006a). It is no exaggeration to say that the future of the profession, including organizations like TESOL International Association, largely depends on the active involvement of classroom teachers. In a recent study of research uptake by foreign language (non-English) teachers, Marsden and Kasprowicz (2017) found that a major reason teachers cited for ignoring published research was that they could not understand it. Clarke (1994) long ago saw this as immensely disabling for the field because "the voices of teachers are subordinated to the voices of others who are less centrally involved in language teaching...[and] occupy positions of greater prestige than classroom language teachers" (p. 13).

A fundamental benefit for teachers of engaging in classroom research is that it forces them to think more deeply about the major issues in the field. This represents a deeper process of professional engagement that serves to raise the status of teachers as they articulate their experiences. In other words, the activity of articulating professional experience validates the authority of teachers as experts in their field. Having more teachers who can speak and write authoritatively about teaching is vital for the direction of educational reform and development of the English language teaching field. Widdowson (1990) articulated this very well:

> Language teaching is often represented as a client activity, and language teachers as consumers of findings that are retailed by research. I believe this is a misrepresentation which denies the nature of teaching as a domain of theory and research in its own right. (p. 47)

The fact is that a lot of teachers are dissatisfied with much of the research published in the field because the studies lack clear practical applications. Marsden and Kasprowicz (2017) found that foreign language teachers in the United Kingdom seldom, if ever, turn to the findings of published research to inform their practice. In the English language teaching field, Borg has conducted a number of surveys on teachers' uptake of published research. For example, he conducted an international survey of 1,160 English as a second language/English as a foreign language teachers and found that 75% reported reading research-related material "sometimes" (Borg, 2010). However, the frequency of "sometimes" and the nature of the teachers' reading was not specified. In addition, studies of academic writing have concluded that, unfortunately, university-based researchers often write in a style that is inaccessible to classroom teachers (e.g., Marsden & Kasprowicz, 2017). This fact has led to researchers in applied linguistics being criticized as elitist and accused of displaying a "lack of generosity" in communicating findings with teachers (Sato & Loewen, 2019, p. 5).

On the other hand, many teachers who have the insights to explain the practical applications of theory are not confident to do their own classroom research and write for publication. Naturally, people fear things that they do not understand. Many English language classroom teachers likely do not understand the research process. The purpose of this book is to demystify classroom research and show teachers that they can and should start researching their teaching. Once the process is transparent, English language teachers often embrace classroom research because of the empowering energy that it generates (Werbner, 2004).

Classroom research is interesting, exciting, and very rewarding. This book aims to help novice teacher-researchers work their way through a classroom research project from the conception of a research idea to the publication of results. In the following three chapters, you will learn how to

- identify topics for classroom research (Chapter 2),

- write research questions (Chapter 2),

- plan a classroom research project (Chapter 3),

- implement a classroom research project and collect data (Chapter 3), and

- publish your results (Chapter 4).

Are you ready to get started? Turn the page to begin your journey as a teacher-researcher.

CHAPTER 2

Getting Started

By hesitating to engage in classroom research, many teachers lose invaluable opportunities to enhance their teaching practice. Casual observations cannot substitute for a carefully planned research project. To novices, classroom research might seem unreasonably difficult, but anyone can do it simply by following some necessary steps.

This chapter will explore these questions:

- What is classroom research?

- How do I develop a research topic?

- How do I write research questions?

Learning does not end once you acquire your credentials and find a teaching job. In fact, this is just the beginning of the real learning experience for a teacher. Inside their classrooms, teachers discover more about education than those outside of classrooms could ever possibly know. Even small-scale discoveries can add valuable insights to current professional discussions on teaching and learning processes. If I suggest to classroom teachers that they should research their practice and publish their findings, however, most practitioners will protest that they cannot do research. How do you feel about researching your teaching?

 REFLECTIVE BREAK
The idea of doing classroom research makes me feel . . .

I once had feelings of inadequacy and concern about my competence as a classroom researcher. Later, as a journal editor, I learned how common these feelings are among classroom practitioners in English language teaching. These concerns are unwarranted, though. The driving force is desire and commitment to learn and improve. In the English language teaching field today, it is more important than ever to advocate for teachers and their students to have a stronger voice in education policies and practices. TESOL International Association (2014) acknowledged this need by stating in their research agenda that there must be "increased emphasis on the agency of teachers as advocates for change inside and outside of their classrooms" (p. 2). One area that needs change in the field is, obviously, generating more published classroom research by English language teaching (ELT) practitioners.

What Is Research?

The classroom is the space where the fun and excitement of learning happen. Many, if not most, English language teachers enter the field because they enjoy teaching. Most of these teachers do not think of themselves as researchers; however, this is a misconception. The fact is that teachers regularly research their practice informally as they struggle with pedagogical issues in their classrooms that they find puzzling. Before reading further, please take a few minutes to carefully consider the following Reflective Break question.

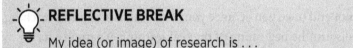

REFLECTIVE BREAK

My idea (or image) of research is . . .

Many novices have misconceptions about research. First, research is not simply making a few quick observations of some phenomenon and coming to a conclusion. Rather, research needs a process that is thorough and systematic. Second, research is not just a chat with knowledgeable colleagues. Research requires an extensive effort over time to collect and analyse evidence. Third, research is not necessarily done in a laboratory on materials whose condition can be precisely controlled. Precision is often lacking in research, in fact, and researchers are typically unsure of what they are looking for. Finally, research is not the neat and tidy manuscript that appears in professional journals and books. The final written product conceals the swirl of doubt, false starts, and frustrating obstacles researchers encounter as they endure the process of doing research. Research that is worthwhile takes sincere commitment. In short, research is a time-consuming, messy, and fun learning process.

Many novices imagine research to be like the kind of studies done in astronomy and physics called *basic research*. This is study done purely for the sake of knowledge. *Applied research*, on the other hand, aims to find solutions to problems. In education, problems are social in nature because they involve human participants. Applied research does not seek to discover general theories, but it is limited by a particular context.

 REFLECTIVE BREAK

List ways in which you have reflected on (or researched) your teaching practice.

In this book, here is how I conceive of research by teachers. First, research is a set of skills people can learn. Because classroom research offers significant professional development benefits, teachers should not be hesitant about researching their teaching. Second, the research methodology should be appropriate to the circumstances. Effective classroom research requires a robust and open-minded view of what constitutes research. Teacher-researchers need to choose a research method or blend of methods based upon the appropriateness. Third, research is a process defined by three key components: a question, problem, puzzle, or hypothesis; data; and analysis and interpretation. To complete the research cycle, results need to be presented in writing or a talk (Nunan & Bailey, 2009).

Language Classroom Research Continuum

The concept of classroom research is often a cover term for "a whole range of research studies on classroom language learning and teaching" (Allwright & Bailey, 1991, p. 2). Table 1 describes activity related to four key terms as approached from *etic* (outsider) or *emic* (insider) perspectives. The obvious point about Table 1 is that teacher research does not exist from the etic perspective. When educators examine their own practice, for example, they adopt the emic perspective. Another interesting point is that classroom research can include either the outsider or the insider view, or both if organized as collaborative research or in professional learning communities.

Table 1. Categories of Second Language Classroom Research

Research/Practice	Etic (Outsider)	Emic (Insider)
Practitioner Research	*Who?* Outside researchers *What?* Things outsiders see *How?* E.g., observation, recording	*Who?* Classroom teachers (students, administrators, etc.) *What?* Things insiders know *How?* E.g., self-evaluation, reflective teaching, teacher research, classroom research
Reflective Practice	*Who?* Outside researchers *What?* Things outsiders see *How?* E.g., stimulated recall	*Who?* Classroom teachers (students, administrators, etc.) *What?* Things insiders know *How?* E.g., journals, lesson reports, action research
Classroom Research	*Who?* Outside researchers, teachers in collaboration *What?* Things outsiders see combined with insider knowledge *How?* E.g., case-study research, survey research, ethnography, narrative, interviews, discourse analysis	*Who?* Classroom teachers, researchers in collaboration (students, administrators, etc.) *What?* Things insiders know combined with researchers' knowledge *How?* E.g., action research, think-aloud protocols, survey research, interviews, discourse analysis, exploratory practice
Teacher Research		*Who?* Classroom teachers *What?* Things insiders know *How?* E.g., action research, autoethnography, narrative, survey research, exploratory practice

This means that a continuum of research perspectives exists in language classroom research.

Practitioner research is the broad umbrella term. It refers to systematic investigations practitioners in any field (e.g., healthcare, engineering, education) conduct on aspects of their daily practices. Ellis (2012) contends that "the value of practitioner research lies more in the process of conducting it than in the product of the research" (p. 26). This point partially explains confusion over terminology because the objectives of second language research that researchers from the outside perform and those of teachers on the inside are usually different. When different outcomes are valued by different types of research practitioners, understandings about what constitutes research can easily become clouded. If questions about values related to classroom research differ between the various research agents, then research methods and related terminology are likely to be affected.

Researchers from the outside will often have purposes such as evaluating teachers or gathering data for later publication. Classroom teachers, however, engage in reflective practice and teacher research typically as feedback into classroom practice with the purpose of professional development aimed at deeper understanding of practice. Naturally, these differing purposes influence the topics of research, the questions asked, the type of input sought, how it is gathered, and how it is analysed and interpreted. Different research processes will often result in very different kinds of output and/or displays of knowledge. In fact, the type of knowledge that is often most valued in higher education research communities can be seen as something alien to practitioners and, therefore, of low value to them. Widdowson (2003) believes many teachers distrust theory because the prestige conferred on it by decision-makers in the field positions theory producers above those who struggle to use theory in practice.

The place of action research in ELT classroom research is important, as is evident in Table 1. Action research is a procedure, or method, for conducting classroom research. Not all classroom research follows the procedures that define action research, so they are not the same. However, action research is always a form of teacher research and classroom research when teachers in their professional contexts conduct it.

What Is Teacher Research?

Stenhouse (1975), through his concept of "the teacher as researcher," paved the way for the contemporary rationale for viewing the classroom as a research site and teachers as research practitioners (e.g., Zeichner & Noffke, 2001). In the ELT field, the work of Allwright and Bailey (1991) was influential for teachers interested in researching their practice. The underlying rationale for teacher research is that by exploring the activity in their own classrooms, teachers better understand their own practice. In this way, teacher research is often linked to professional development.

The defining feature of teacher research is the researcher. In other words, the agent who conducts the research is the classroom teacher. This dominant variable is constant and is independent of research location and research methods. Definitions of teacher research commonly describe self-initiated "inquiry conducted by teachers in their own professional contexts" systematically (Borg, 2013, p. 8).

What Is Classroom Research?

Classroom research involves doing research in school settings about teaching and learning. Descriptions of school settings can range a great deal, of course, from private lessons to large university lectures. Physical settings also vary widely, and, because of digital communications, today a classroom can be a virtual setting with participants who are miles apart in actual physical distance. I define classroom research as a process of investigating puzzling aspects of teaching, learning, and interaction in the classroom that is undertaken through a systematic process of data collection, analysis, and publication of results by teachers who want to better understand their professional practice.

Classroom-based research is also referred to as classroom-centered research. According to Allwright (1983), classroom-centered research "simply tries to investigate what happens inside the classroom when learners and teachers come together" (p. 191). Allwright explained further that the main concern of classroom-centered/classroom-based research is the process and sequence of lessons, interaction between participants, and activity related to teaching and learning. Insiders or outsiders can conduct classroom research (Table 1), and as a result, it is closely related to the broad category of practitioner research, where practitioners are people who are members of any professional field.

There are quantitative and qualitative approaches to conducting research. Underlying *quantitative* studies is the idea that reality can be broken down into parts and studied, whereas *qualitative* researchers accept that reality can only be studied holistically. Quantitative research begins with a definite research question or hypothesis, but in qualitative studies the research question often evolves and is clarified during the research process. Of course, quantitative research involves statistical data analysis. In qualitative research studies, however, collected data is analysed through interpretation and categorization.

Researchers should select a research method based upon the needs of the situation. Most ELT practitioners will likely engage in qualitative research, so that is the focus in this book. It is advisable, however, for classroom researchers to include some quantitative elements in their study if possible. I fully agree with Nunan and Bailey (2009) that blended approaches to research design often produce superior results. The number of mixed methods classroom research studies has greatly increased over the past 10 years.

Are you ready to begin? Or are you still an English language teacher who thinks of research negatively? Perhaps you think of research only as large-scale studies done by outside "experts" who will be happy to report to you how you should be teaching. Maybe you just need some guidance to help you get started.

Finding a Research Focus

The first step in any research project—getting and clarifying ideas for classroom research—is normally the most difficult and tedious. Here, at the very start, is often the place where novices give up. Why? When they have difficulty finding a clear research focus, many teachers get frustrated and confused, which leads them to mistakenly believe that they are not able to do classroom research. Often, researchers begin with some vague area of interest and think for quite a long time about what in particular interests them about this area. After much careful thought, including a good deal of background reading, a research question (or questions) is eventually formulated.

 REFLECTIVE BREAK

What general area of your classroom experience currently interests or puzzles you most?

For the Reflective Break, you may have listed any number of things, for instance, something about your own teaching (e.g., how I introduce tasks). Or you might be more interested in something related to student participation (e.g., why some students often appear to be off task). Rather than a concern about tasks in a generic sense, you might find it more useful to focus on a particular skill area (e.g., reading, writing, speaking, listening, study skills) or issues related to grouping, classroom management, or assessment. Look at recent issues of English language education journals to see what other people are researching. Also, if you have a program book or link from a conference you attended recently, skim over the titles for ideas. In fact, going to conferences can be an ideal way to spark your imagination for classroom research, so by all means attend conferences and network.

A technique that has helped me refine ideas for classroom research is *focusing circles* (Edge, 2002). Draw a large circle with a small circle in the centre like a donut. Inside the small circle write a general topic from your practice that interests you—testing, for example. Then, break the general topic down into more specific parts and write these points inside separate segments of the larger circle. After this, choose one of the segments to focus on and write it in the middle of a new donut circle. Once again, break this topic down into smaller components. Repeat this sequence with a new circle. After you do this seriously for three or four circles, "something very interesting happens. What had been a topic... starts to sound more like an action....Once we have identified it, we can formulate a plan of action" (Edge, 2002, p. 103). Freeman (1998) outlines a similar technique adapted from Peter Elbow called *loop writing* that might appeal to teachers having trouble finding a research focus.

At this beginning stage of the research process, do not discard any ideas you think of as possible topics for inquiry. It is important to take some time to think and write down *all* your ideas. One of your general ideas can surely be developed into a specific research focus over time. When you are ready, think carefully about one of your general topic areas by reflecting on the questions in Table 2.

Table 2. Refining Your Research Focus

Question	Answer
Why are you interested in this topic?	
How does this topic impact your teaching?	
Can you think of a particular incident from your own teaching practice related to this topic?	
Try to define the specific issue of this incident as clearly as possible.	

Formulating a Research Question

Once you have a research topic, you will need to write at least one research question. Clearly written research questions are extremely important because they give your research project a direction that you can plan around. Think carefully about your own beliefs of how one should teach because a good research question is one that you form while acknowledging its bias. MacKay (2006) wisely advises classroom researchers initially to clarify beliefs about teaching and learning so that they can understand the biases that underlie their research design. Teachers all teach through a framework created by their own particular set of beliefs about pedagogy and learning.

How can you write a strong research question? If you have difficulty formulating a concise research question, begin with a general question, and investigate recent research (i.e., within the past 5 years) on this topic. As you read the relevant studies, practice active reading by taking notes and posing questions related to your own teaching experience. It may help you most to read action research or classroom research case studies done by practitioners (e.g., Bailey & Nunan, 1996; Dawson, 2017; Edge, 2001; Farrell, 2006; Stewart, 2017). Seeing how other teachers have gone about planning their classroom research can be a powerful motivation because it illuminates pathways.

Besides reading the work of colleagues whom you might not know, the rewards of talking about your classroom research interests with colleagues you do know can be tremendous. Find a trusted colleague and discuss your research ideas at length. As a novice teacher-researcher, I eagerly sought out colleagues with whom I could collaborate on research projects. I find collaborative research to be the most rewarding.

If you are still not able to formulate a satisfactory research question, then you might try keeping a teaching journal for several weeks. It does not have to be a comprehensive diary of your practice. What you are looking for are puzzling aspects of your practice. This means that you should note any questions that come to mind while you are teaching. Bring your journal into your classes and write questions or points of interest during lessons, if possible. Later, you can think more deeply about these questions.

Freeman (1998) illustrates the qualities of a "research-able" question. He defines good questions as "open-ended [with] multiple directions and responses" (p. 63). A good research question should be aimed at a broad understanding of the issue. Classroom research is done in a specific context, but to contribute to the ELT field as a whole, results should be examined from a wider perspective. Consider the example in the following Reflective Break.

REFLECTIVE BREAK

Can you improve the focus of the following as a research question?

What types of writing activities do my students most enjoy?

The research question example in the Reflective Break is a good starting question that just needs a sharper focus. Rather than simply asking what types of activities your students like, you can widen your inquiry by looking at specific writing activities and asking how they help (or hinder) the proficiency of your students. A teacher may, for instance, try to answer three questions—what students like, why they like these activities, and how the activities help students to improve.

REFLECTIVE BREAK

Are there any problems with the following question as the basis for a research topic?

How does peer feedback improve student writing?

The strength of this research question example is that it states a specific phenomenon for research: peer feedback. The problem is that it starts from a basic assumption: that peer feedback improves student writing. Alternatively, a teacher-researcher might ask, "Does peer feedback improve student writing?" A teacher might try to dig deeper into the issue, however, and ask something like, "What kinds of peer feedback strategies do my students use and why?"

The crucial point about doing research is to get started. Do your best to write the clearest research question possible, but do not delay beginning your project in an endless search for a perfectly posed question. Classroom inquiry is an ongoing process for teachers, and once you enter the data-gathering and analysis stages, you may find that your real focus emerges. This is the nature of social research. Novice researchers must keep in mind that research is messy. Do not hesitate to reformulate your research question as your understanding deepens. Keep in mind that there is no "perfect" research. Your aim should be to do the best that you can do at any particular point in time.

 REFLECTIVE BREAK

Write a research question based on your own interest. Your question(s) can help you simulate the classroom research process in the next chapter.

Data Collection and Analysis

Now that you have a satisfactory research question, it is time to carefully plan the implementation of your project. This involves systematically thinking through each step of your research plan. This chapter explores the following questions:

- How do I plan my classroom research project?

- What kind of data should I collect?

- How do I collect and analyse data?

The core of research is gathering data. First, you need to consider the types of data that can help you investigate your research questions. Next, you have to make a concrete plan for collecting the data. Finally, you must decide how to analyse the data. Good planning is crucial to the success of your project. Think through your plan a number of times and explain it step-by-step to two or three colleagues before you take action. You might begin by answering the questions in Table 3.

Table 3. Planning Your Data Collection and Analysis

Questions	Answers
What kinds of data will respond to my research question?	

(continued)

Table 3 (cont.)

Questions	Answers
What are ways that these data can be collected?	
How can I collect this kind of data in my classroom?	
What kind of preparations do I need to do to collect these data?	
How long will it take to gather the data? (i.e., how often will I gather the data and for how many classes?)	
How can I analyse the data? (This may require more reading of the classroom research literature.)	

Source: Adapted from Freeman (1998, p. 74)

The data collection methods in Table 4 were chosen based on anticipated potential ease for novice classroom researchers to collect. The following section explores collection and analysis methods for some of these types of data.

Table 4. Overview of Selected Data Types

Data Collection Techniques	Description
Audio or video recording	Recordings capture classroom activities, including verbal information (as well as nonverbal with video). General class information, student interactions, or actions of the teacher can be recorded for later analysis.
Student or teacher journals	Journals are sometimes shaped as diaries or learning logs, depending on their purpose. They can be created by teachers and students to record reflections, thoughts, and observations focused on lessons, tasks, or general thoughts.
Lesson plans	Lesson plans follow a template that includes objectives, materials, pedagogical sequence, and expected outcomes.
Field notes	Field notes are taken by the teacher at regular points during a lesson or when particular observations or questions inspire notation. The notes can be organized in a general frame or guided by predetermined questions.

(continued)

Table 4 (cont.)

Data Collection Techniques	Description
Archival documents	These are items such as student work, test scores, evaluations, administrative policies, email communication, minutes of meetings, and other documents linked to teaching and learning in classes.
Interviews	Interviews are oral or written (e.g., email) interactions that can be open ended or structured. The latter type is structured around questions intended to gather particular sorts of information, and the former is guided by more general thematic topics.
Questionnaires	Questionnaires are instruments for gathering factual, behavioural, and attitudinal data from respondents. Questions can be both open ended and close ended. A Likert scale that presents a consistent range of response categories is commonly used with close-ended questions.

General Areas of Classroom Research Inquiry

There is not enough space in this short book to cover all the methods of gathering and analysing data. To simplify the process, I introduce five general areas of inquiry into teaching and learning and outline how you might collect data for each. As you work through each area, consider how you would approach organizing the research.

Teacher Actions

This type of classroom research focuses on pedagogy and activity by teachers in the classroom during lessons. By looking at Table 4, you should be able to select some possible techniques of data collection. Lesson plans and field notes are two possibilities. In addition, teachers can video-record lessons to observe themselves.

The type of data you would generate through field notes and lesson plans depends on your advanced planning. By creating a lesson plan with adequate white space, you can easily write observations focused on your plan versus implementation, your thoughts, and reactions of students. If you use a computer in lessons, then you can write comments directly on your screen in real time. The validity of your results depends on your diligence and consistency, so set your procedures and stick to them. Record your observations as close to the actual event as possible.

Teacher Thoughts

Rather than focusing just on the teacher's actions in the classroom, researching teacher thoughts would involve deeper reflection about what the teacher is doing in lessons and why. The straightforward way to collect data for this type of reflective practice is through the use of a journal or diary. It is also possible to record a lesson and reflect on it later through what is called stimulated recall, but this method depends heavily on memory, so it is not preferred.

For a journal, you need a special notebook or a computer. A journal must have regular entries and can be open ended based on a particular theme of inquiry, or more directed with predetermined questions you respond to regularly over a period of time.

Student Actions

This type of classroom research would be used to discover what your students do or say in lessons. Take some time now to reflect on possible data collection techniques.

 REFLECTIVE BREAK

How would you suggest data be collected for classroom research on student actions?

A teacher could choose to write field notes to gather data on student actions, and these notes can take different forms. For instance, you might write annotations directly into a lesson plan in real time or as soon as possible after the activity. Recordings can be made of the whole class, a group of students, or a particular student. Finally, you could conduct interviews of some or all students.

If you choose to do video or audio recordings, be sure that you are very familiar with the equipment. Do more than one test of the equipment and check that the power is full and microphones are switched on. Students will behave differently when recording equipment is placed in the classroom, so it is advisable to bring the equipment in several times to have students feel comfortable with it. On the day you want to record, simply turn it on casually. If you need clear sound of student interaction, you might require special microphones or the space to isolate groups. Later, you will need to transcribe the recording.

Student Thoughts

This type of general inquiry would focus the teacher-researcher on what students think about their own learning, ability, and their activity in the classroom. Once again, please consider possible choices of data collection techniques from Table 4.

REFLECTIVE BREAK

How would you suggest data be collected for classroom research on student thoughts?

To discover what students are thinking about their studies, diaries or journals are often used in classroom research. Other data-gathering techniques could include questionnaires and interviews.

When you design a questionnaire, be sure to write short, straightforward questions. Also keep in mind the language level of students. If a questionnaire is too difficult to complete, your data will be poor. Writing questions in the students' home language is often a good choice for homogeneous groups of students at the beginning level. Include at least some open-ended questions in your questionnaire and test it before you conduct your study.

Student Learning

This type of inquiry would investigate what students have learned. Interviews and questionnaires are possible instruments for data collection. Teachers could also collect student work and test results to analyse. Once again, students could provide feedback about their learning through journals, diaries, or learning logs—a type of journal directed by a predetermined set of questions.

Samples of student work could be compared with the thoughts of students about learning tasks, for example. For this kind of project, a learning log could be used to gather student perceptions of tasks. With student journals and questionnaires, a major concern is the honesty of responses because students might give responses they believe will please teachers. For this reason, anonymous instruments should be used whenever possible.

Data Collection Issues

The descriptions of the five general areas of classroom research inquiry should help novice teacher-researchers in several ways. First, there are many possible directions for inquiries in classroom research. Some research involves more reflective data, and other projects rely on observational data related to classroom interaction. Second, the data collection technique needs to be one that best addresses the research question. Beyond this, however, it is crucial to be realistic about your ability to collect the data. Do you have time built into lessons for this purpose? Do your students need to be prepared in some way before the project begins? Related questions address how much data you need and how often you should collect it. Sometimes quantity can overtake quality, especially if you feel pressured and become hurried and careless. Proceed with care and gather data thoughtfully.

How robust or sturdy is your data set? The concept of *triangulation* is used in architecture to describe design features that enable a structure to support its weight. When teachers think of data triangulation, they may imagine examining a phenomenon from more than one angle. Classroom researchers should not rely on one type of data for analysis (e.g., student journal entries) but should investigate their research question from two or three different perspectives on the same phenomenon (e.g., including questionnaires or transcripts of student–student classroom interaction). To do this, you need to plan to collect different types of data related to your inquiry. Viewing your inquiry from multiple perspectives is crucial for gaining a holistic picture of your classroom (see Quirke, 2001; also, Stewart, 2006b, for a multilayered approach).

Moving From Plan Into Action

A comprehensive and systematic plan is essential to guide your research project. Unexpected things happen regularly in classrooms. Although no amount of preparation can prevent surprises, having a solid action plan will give you the confidence to improvise. When things do not go as expected, novices might get the impression that they are not conducting their research correctly, but if you have made your plan with adequate care, you must follow through on it. If you need to alter your data collection for some reason, be sure that you do so in a systematic way. Data collection is the heart of the research process, so it has to be well organized.

Before you implement your classroom research plan, be sure to go over it one last time very carefully. Do you have all of the equipment and materials that you need for this project? Do you know how to operate it? It might be best to do a trial of your procedures in the classroom when it is empty a week or so before the actual event. Remember to enjoy your foray into classroom research. You will find it exhilarating (Werbner, 2004). While collecting data, try to observe the process and make notes of your thoughts about what takes place. Immediately afterward, an early first analysis of the data can give you ideas about ways to analyse the data further.

If your project requires gathering data from your students, you must explain your project to students and get their permission to use their work, images, or words. In some contexts, it will be necessary to first get your project approved by administrators. Be sensitive, use common sense, and conduct your research project ethically.

Seeking Meaning Out of the Mess

Analysing qualitative data resembles building sand castles at the beach: Just when you think you have created something reasonably solid, it begins to crumble before your eyes. The four key types of data analysis can be called labelling, categorizing, finding patterns or themes, and displaying. Data first appears as one big confusing mass of information. For it to be useful, you must organize that mass. For example, participants and entries could be labelled or coded. To assist them, teacher-researchers can borrow labels from previous studies, or they might choose to create their own labels. Often, in qualitative research, labels emerge from the data during analysis. Once the parts are named, the teacher-researcher needs to reassemble the data in chunks that make sense by grouping similar information. It is not uncommon during data analysis for researchers to think there is nothing significant. You need to go over your data many times before you can see the significant patterns.

Next, categories must be linked somehow by finding relationships between them. In fact, finding significant patterns and connections is the main task of analysis. Last, the researcher needs to draw or map out the interpretation of the data somehow. This is an important step that helps the teacher-researcher visualize the larger meaning of the whole. These meaning maps are normally redrawn as your understanding of the data develops. Sharing your meaning map and explaining it to colleagues will help you to clarify it.

Finally, classroom research needs to be based on current theoretical knowledge and practice recorded in the research literature. Read current studies and situate your research project within contemporary knowledge about teaching and learning. Novices might find comfort in replicating previous studies when beginning classroom research. This is perfectly acceptable, but take care to customize the research design to reflect your situation.

The next chapter concerns what you do with your research results. One very important step is to connect your findings to key ideas in the research literature. Your classroom research inquiry must relate thoughtfully to previous studies and theories. This is how you connect your practice to the larger issues of general discussion in the profession. Studies that fail to do this are normally rejected by editors.

 REFLECTIVE BREAK

- Reexamine the research question you wrote at the end of Chapter 2 and decide which of the five general types of classroom research inquiry is the best fit.

- Next, review Table 3 and Table 4 and create a detailed data collection plan.

CHAPTER 4

Publishing Your Findings

How Do I Prepare My Ideas for Publication?

Whether your publication is a conference presentation or a full manuscript, the most important thing you must do when approaching a publication venue is to take note of the topics, writing style, and requirements you find in that publication. Once you identify a venue that seems like a fit for your work, carefully craft your ideas to match the publication. The biggest mistake that novice writers make, besides choosing inappropriate publication venues, is not following the submission guidelines. You must follow the guidelines if you hope to have your work considered for publication. If your submission is not presented in a complete and professional manner, the editor will simply return it and ask that it be resubmitted according to the submission guidelines, or they may reject it altogether without an explanation.

Conference Proposals

Conferences are organized around themes, so your proposal must address the theme. Do not simply take an old proposal you have written and add a sentence or two related to the theme. Read the call for proposals carefully. Address the conference theme in your proposal and include some of the buzzwords highlighted in the conference call. Revise your proposal a number of times and ask a couple of colleagues to critique it. Begin writing it early so that you have plenty of time to revise before the submission deadline.

Conferences typically invite proposals for papers, demonstrations, workshops, panels, posters, and audio-visual media presentations. Select the presentation style that displays your work best. Papers, for example, tend to be short lectures with minimal audience participation, whereas workshops need to include audience tasks, as well as time for contributions from participants. Many first-time presenters seem to prefer giving poster presentations. Though this may appear to be a less stressful type of presentation, great care needs to be taken to create a professional looking poster with a self-explanatory message. This is not so easy to achieve.

After deciding on the presentation style you feel comfortable with, pay specific attention to the time allotted for your presentation. Then, with this time limit in mind, make a basic outline of the flow of your session from introduction to conclusion. Do you want to allow some time for questions from the audience at the end? Do you have enough time to give adequate background to help the audience understand your project? Which pieces of data will you present and in what format? Do you have video of student interaction and permission to show it? These are just some of the questions you will need to consider as you plan your proposal. I advise you from the start to imagine that your proposal will be accepted and then at the outset to think systematically about the steps needed to present your information clearly.

Many novices underestimate the time it takes to present their classroom research. This unrealistic planning leads presenters to pack in too much information, which in turn causes them to present in a rushed manner. Realistic planning, including doing a timed practice session after your proposal is in fact accepted, should help you to avoid this situation. Design and deliver your presentation for the audience, not for you. Lay things out clearly so that people unfamiliar with your context can easily follow your reasoning. Try to have no more than 20 slides and be sure that slides present information visually, using keywords. The saying "less is more" is definitely fitting when managing presentation content.

Proposals for conferences have word limits, so make sure that you do not exceed the limit. Remember that the volunteers who vet the proposals may have to read hundreds of them. If your proposal looks unprofessional and is too long, it will likely be rejected straight off. Also, make sure you know the deadline for submissions and try to send your proposal in a little early. You should get a message from the organizers confirming that your proposal was received.

REFLECTIVE BREAK

Do an internet search for English language education conferences and examine the theme and proposal guidelines for one or two conferences that interest you.

Professional Association Newsletters

Professional associations generally have special interest groups, or interest sections. As of 2023, TESOL International Association, for instance, has 20 interest sections, including Adult Education, Intercultural Communication, Social Responsibility, English as a Foreign Language, and "Nonnative" English Speaker Teachers. Each interest section produces a newsletter. For novices, these newsletters are ideal venues for gaining valuable experience writing and editing. In addition to these communities, there are currently 10 professional learning networks listed on the TESOL International Association website, including Career Path Development, Environmental Responsibility, Arts and Creativity, and Assessment Issues. Each of these networks is an informal discussion group organized by members with similar interests. Informal discussion groups can introduce teachers to a network of concerned professionals who can provide useful support and advice.

REFLECTIVE BREAK

Which interest sections or networks supported by an association you belong to most interest you?

Interest sections welcome new members, and mentorship is common in these specialized groups of professionals. As a novice teacher-researcher with an interest in writing for professional purposes, you should contact the editor of your interest section newsletter. Of course, you must first read several issues of the newsletter, including the most recent issues. Find out the topics of current discussion and consider whether you can add something meaningful. Also, carefully note the writing style of the articles and the various columns or sections in the newsletter. Read the submission guidelines with care and be alert for any calls for submissions (most importantly, special topic issues).

Find out who the editor is and sell your idea. When you approach an editor, do so formally at first. Although today's social media networks have encouraged a tone of familiarity, do not make an overly friendly, informal approach to others in the profession. This means using the salutation *Dear* and the surname of the person together with *Mr.*, *Ms.*, *Professor*, or *Dr.* as appropriate. If, after the first communication, the editor wishes to communicate in a more informal way using first names, then you can change the register of your correspondence. However, it is best not to use language that is too friendly unless you know the person well.

Journal Articles

There are many online journals in need of submissions, so they present novices with excellent opportunities. Because the number of journals continues to grow, many do not receive the volume of manuscripts they would like. In short, the English language teaching publishing world is waiting for contributions from practitioners like you. All you need to do is submit the best quality manuscript you can to the right publication.

In the hierarchy of academic publishing, full-length articles and book chapters are right at the top, along with writing a reference book. This section focuses on manuscripts for feature articles, but many journals invite submissions of teaching tips and shorter discussions of current teaching and theoretical issues. These shorter submission categories are often more accessible to novices. After seeing your teaching tip in print, you will gain confidence to write something longer in the future.

To get your manuscript published in a journal, you must submit something of quality. Remember, good writing is hard work, even in this era of chatbots. Figure 1 is a checklist to help authors produce the best submissions possible and have their manuscripts published.

Journal editors, book editors, and reviewers are sometimes volunteers who juggle editing and numerous other professional obligations, such as preparing and teaching lessons. Because they are busy professionals like you, they will not want to spend valuable time trying to decode your message. Write using active voice in a straightforward style. It is your job to clearly explain your classroom research project and why it matters. In short, you need to sell your manuscript to the editor and reviewers. If you have the resources, you might consider hiring a professional editor to read your paper with a critical eye. This can potentially give your manuscript an advantage over the competition because many initial submissions are poorly written.

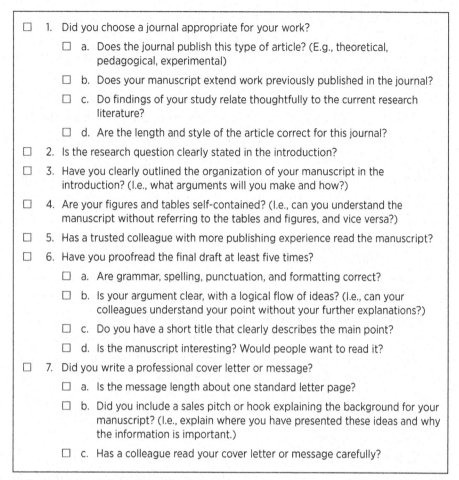

1. Did you choose a journal appropriate for your work?
   - a. Does the journal publish this type of article? (E.g., theoretical, pedagogical, experimental)
   - b. Does your manuscript extend work previously published in the journal?
   - c. Do findings of your study relate thoughtfully to the current research literature?
   - d. Are the length and style of the article correct for this journal?
2. Is the research question clearly stated in the introduction?
3. Have you clearly outlined the organization of your manuscript in the introduction? (I.e., what arguments will you make and how?)
4. Are your figures and tables self-contained? (I.e., can you understand the manuscript without referring to the tables and figures, and vice versa?)
5. Has a trusted colleague with more publishing experience read the manuscript?
6. Have you proofread the final draft at least five times?
   - a. Are grammar, spelling, punctuation, and formatting correct?
   - b. Is your argument clear, with a logical flow of ideas? (I.e., can your colleagues understand your point without your further explanations?)
   - c. Do you have a short title that clearly describes the main point?
   - d. Is the manuscript interesting? Would people want to read it?
7. Did you write a professional cover letter or message?
   - a. Is the message length about one standard letter page?
   - b. Did you include a sales pitch or hook explaining the background for your manuscript? (I.e., explain where you have presented these ideas and why the information is important.)
   - c. Has a colleague read your cover letter or message carefully?

Figure 1. Submission Checklist for Authors

It is important to remember that research is a story that follows a narrative style. Tell the story of your classroom research project with clarity and in an engaging style. Do not turn off readers with convoluted explanations; make it interesting. Know your point and state it with clarity. Make sure as well that your headings and subheadings help readers to comprehend your points and act as informative signposts illuminating your argument in a cohesive flow. Also, read and become familiar with the journal you are submitting to and tailor your writing to suit audience expectations.

Other Venues

Keep in mind that professional associations run on the energy of volunteers, so volunteering can help you gain experience in academic publishing. Once you get a little experience giving presentations and writing, you should consider volunteering as a manuscript reviewer or proofreader. Journals, particularly small local journals, are typically short of staff. New volunteers are normally sought eagerly for positions in association interest sections as well. After becoming familiar with an interest section over 1 or 2 years, it is worthwhile to volunteer for an administrative position. This can be very rewarding work. In addition, conference organizers seek out volunteers to vet presentation proposals. This is an excellent way to see how proposals are written. You will quickly see the difference between well-written proposals and marginal or poorly written ones. In short, becoming a volunteer allows you to pull back the curtain and gain an insider's perspective on academic publishing.

For many novices, writing reviews of books, websites, software, and other teaching materials is a comfortable entry threshold into the world of academic publication. Reviews are normally short, at 500–800 words in length. This word count is both a blessing and a challenge because, although it requires much less writing than an article, it forces the writer to describe the material being reviewed very precisely. The two big advantages for novices in writing reviews are, first, you become skilled at explaining your point with particular clarity and, second, you gain motivation to continue academic writing after seeing your work published. Also, reviews tend to follow a template that may make entry into writing for publication more attainable for writers who have acquired English as an additional language.

Remember that a review is a short overview and therefore cannot possibly cover all aspects of any work. This means that you can only touch on the most important points. A review is a description, but it should be critical in nature. That is, you need to describe and evaluate the features of the material. To do this well, keep the intended audience of the material in mind as you write your review. Is the material suited to the target audience?

Many teacher-researchers begin publishing by submitting reviews and writing for professional newsletters. Learning how to write manuscripts that get accepted for publication simply takes experience and determination. Once you feel ready, you can submit longer manuscripts to academic journals.

 REFLECTIVE BREAK

Have you read or used some newly published materials for teaching or professional reference in the past year that you could review?

A Word on Plagiarism

Journal editors today routinely complain about submissions of plagiarized material. The tip of the iceberg reveals a disturbing trend where people boldly copy the work of others in whole or in part and submit it as their own. This is not an appropriate or recommended path into the world of academic publishing. Though there is pressure to publish, deliberate plagiarism is more of a path toward career curtailment than advancement. You can get published if you really want to, but you must put in the required work. The reward for all of your effort is seeing your article in print.

What if My Manuscript Is Rejected?

The real question here is not *if*, but what to do *when* you get a rejection (Casanave & Vandrick, 2003). Becoming a writer certainly means that you need to learn how to deal with rejection. Academic manuscripts are normally checked by no fewer than two anonymous reviewers. These anonymous reviewers are people who volunteer from the ranks of teachers. In other words, they are people like you and me. Of course, reviewers vary according to depth of knowledge and skill, but each reviewer will spend a good deal of time considering the strengths and weaknesses of your paper. Some reviewers are better at mentoring and nurturing than others, but even with the most supportive reviewer, you need to be prepared for criticism. Criticism of work you have toiled over for weeks can be difficult to read, but the majority of manuscripts submitted will require revision. If you find the comments upsetting, calmly step away from them for a time. Return to them after a few days and analyse them with care and a degree of objectivity. What are the reviewers positive about, and what do they recommend for improving your manuscript? Make a detailed checklist and consider each point thoughtfully. You can disagree with reviewers and do not have to make all of the changes they suggest. If you decide not to make some changes, you should have good reasons. When you submit your revision, include separate lists of the changes you made and did not make. In the latter list, include your reasons.

Reviewers and editors are colleagues who should be interested in helping you write the very best manuscript possible at a given time. I can honestly say that every single time I have submitted a manuscript, the reviewer comments have helped me to improve my writing. Of course, this is always after my bruised ego has healed. Do not take the comments of reviewers personally. Instead, learn from them because they definitely will help you to improve your writing. If you are serious about writing for publication, you need patience, flexibility, and humility (Hargittai, 2011).

 REFLECTIVE BREAK

If you have had manuscripts or proposals rejected in the past, what reasons were given?

It might sound odd, but starting a research writing project is perhaps more important than finishing because many would-be teacher-researchers never get past the stage of conception. Ideas may come to mind but can stall at the execution stage. Beyond that, few things are more dreaded by many people than staring at a blank page while trying to write something. But writing something, anything, is what you must do. If you do not start, you will never finish. Your ideas may not be presented as elegantly as you would like initially; however, that explains why revision is the essential task of good writers.

Protocol in academic publication is for a manuscript to be submitted to only one publication at a time (i.e., no simultaneous submissions). The wait can be trying, but you need to follow this rule. Sometimes after rejection by one journal, you have to shop a manuscript around. In this case, take the reviewer advice seriously and rework your manuscript before you submit it to another journal. It is not a good idea to simply send off the rejected manuscript again without changes. Most important, do not give up on your work if you believe in it. Instead, revise the manuscript to fit the requirements of the new target journal and be prepared to do this more than once for some manuscripts. It is important to understand that colleagues who get published in the field all experience rejection regularly and put in a great deal of time revising their work.

CHAPTER 5

Continuing With Classroom Research

After making your first presentation and seeing your name in print, you will no doubt be motivated to continue contributing to the field, and continue you should. This final chapter offers some advice about how to stay motivated and reinforces key points made in the book.

This chapter explores these questions:

- How can teacher-researchers stay motivated to continue with classroom research?

- What should English language teachers take away from this book?

Consider in the following Reflective Break where you began as a teacher-researcher and where you want to go.

REFLECTIVE BREAK

What have been your motivations to date for beginning classroom research? How might you sustain these motivating forces?

For most teachers, the reward they get from knowing more about their students and their pedagogy is what keeps them pushing forward to learn more. Of course, professional development is an obligation for all professionals, but we can all fall short at times. Burnout is one major reason for falling short. Yes, you can overdo it when it comes to reflective practice and classroom research, so engage in it selectively. Do not research your teaching practice constantly. After completing a project, take a needed break and plan future interventions into your classroom with care.

Dick Allwright (2005) has long been concerned about "the high risk of burnout associated with current proposals for teacher-based classroom research" (p. 27). He believes, quite reasonably, that if teachers view classroom research as something too demanding, they will not attempt it. In response, Allwright developed seven general principles for educators interested in exploring puzzling aspects of their teaching and learning practices together with their students. He calls this approach exploratory practice (Hanks, 2017). The aim is to open a natural integration of enquiry into classroom activities to make classroom research sustainable (see the Appendix for an example).

In addition to exploratory practice, a sustainable way to maintain your enthusiasm for professional development is collaboration with colleagues. Teachers who want to better understand their practice and their students through classroom research have to overcome a number of obstacles (e.g., time, experience/expertise, resources, and support). For novices, a good way to start would be to work with a more experienced colleague.

 REFLECTIVE BREAK

Which colleagues could you approach for professional development collaboration? How would you do this?

Find colleagues who you can work with on teaching issues either at your institution or elsewhere. It is a cliché, but two heads *are* better than one. Consider trying the cooperative development approach of Edge (2002) as a way to maintain enthusiasm. Cooperative development is a systematic approach for colleagues to talk about their teaching. More than that, it aims to extend the talk of an individual teacher so that their ideas can be clarified. This is done through a supportive colleague who uses prescribed techniques to listen to and help focus the talk of a peer. Once focused, the ultimate aim of this talk is to reveal to the teacher issues they deem as the most urgent to their professional development and take action on them. Edge offers teachers a collaborative model for clarifying classroom research plans. The ultimate goal is to empower teachers through professional actions based on their own understanding of their teaching situation. The defining feature of Edge's approach is the active use of colleagues as sounding boards who help an individual teacher formulate their ideas. In the end, self-development requires the support of other teachers.

The following example, from Thailand, is instructional. Maneekhao engaged in action research for the first time for both professional development and to contribute to the university's curriculum renewal (Maneekhao & Todd, 2001). She worked with a mentor-colleague and kept a research journal. She was open about her lack of knowledge of the process: "I had no idea what research is like, how it is useful and did not want to know either" (p. 58). She was also honest about her sense of fear and confusion while conducting her research: "I am not a genius…it is a blur" (p. 60). Her feelings match descriptions of the research process in the literature as "endless, painful, boring and time-consuming" (Brown & Rodgers, 2002). After completing her action research, things looked different to Maneekhao as she was able to step back and see the whole picture. She discovered that, thankfully, research is not endless, although it is time-consuming and somewhat painful. However, when a teacher sees a project through to completion, something emerges from the fog of the struggle. She gained some clarity and learned that research is not boring because it tells practitioners a lot about what they are doing and why, and how it affects students and teachers themselves. In short, systematic classroom research can be a career-changing experience.

The Classroom Research Learning Loop

Teaching and classroom research go hand in hand. Teaching activity raises the questions for investigation, and the classroom provides the setting. Classroom research then should, as far as possible, be a kind of investigation that uses data generated in regular exercises. In addition, results should feed into teaching practice and make it more appropriate. This is a virtuous circle that builds professionalism, which, in turn, empowers individual English language teachers while it unites, strengthens, and raises the profile of the field as a whole.

Wharton (2008) has extensively researched the challenges faced by classroom teachers who desire to establish a dual identity as teacher and writer about teaching. She contends that

> individuals who are willing to take on this dual identity provide the profession with an invaluable resource, that is, an accumulation

of accounts written by people with expertise *both* in the practice of [English language] teaching, and in the theoretical practice of writing about it. (p. 228)

No doubt some teachers reading this book will still question their ability to do a "proper" classroom research project. This raises one of the big questions in the field: What is proper or "appropriate" research design? Two prominent researchers (Holliday, 2004; Shohamy, 2004) asked this question in the pages of *TESOL Quarterly* two decades ago. They claimed that the boundaries of research are crumbling so that today many possibilities exist for blending research methods. This indicates that descriptions of teaching practice should be valued more in English language teaching (ELT) research. In her critique of the *correct* structure for reporting research in ELT, Shohamy (2004) concluded that in our digital age, "it would be useful if research guidelines encouraged researchers to present their results in more innovative ways" (p. 729). In short, the doors are now opening to teachers to contribute to the discussions in the literature. The path to enter into these discussions is classroom research.

What makes the classroom research learning loop so important for ELT research is positioning. Teaching and research are very different activities (see Ellis, 2012). Teaching is a practical act that involves implementing the technical knowledge base of research through a process of reshaping based on the teacher's experiential knowledge. Interaction in a classroom is the filter through which technical and practical knowledge are interchangeably distilled to create opportunity for learning. To further our understanding of teaching and learning processes, classroom teachers should do more to raise their awareness of the processes that teaching entails. It is no exaggeration to claim that the classroom is the crucible where this complex interaction occurs, and teachers are the professionals best positioned to articulate that interaction to others in the field.

Like all experiential things in life, after you do it once, classroom research does not seem so daunting. Perhaps this research phobia is ingrained because by default, even in ELT, teachers think of research as large-scale empirical studies. It is long past time to raise the profile of teachers' experiential knowledge in the research literature, and it is the duty of classroom teachers to do this. This is a task that is worthwhile and well within the capabilities of teachers to accomplish. But to succeed, you have to put aside your self-doubt, take the plunge, and start.

I hope that many teachers will use the ideas in this book to join in the current professional discussions in the field of ELT. The field needs to hear much more from classroom practitioners about what they do in lessons. Remember, when it comes to teaching language to people, you are an expert. Share your expertise with others in the field. The ELT community is waiting for you to join the professional conversation.

Publication Venues Suggested for Novices

ELT Journal

https://academic.oup.com/eltj/pages/General_Instructions

Invites submissions which deal with a wide range of ELT issues

English Teaching Forum

americanenglish.state.gov/submission-guidelines

Publishes articles and teaching techniques for teachers of English as a foreign language (EFL)

Language Magazine

www.languagemagazine.com/guidelines-for-submissions-to-language -magazine

Accepts submissions of articles up to 2,500 words for English and other languages

The Language Teacher

jalt-publications.org/tlt/submissions

Accepts submissions of manuscripts on topics related to teaching and learning in Japan

RELC Journal

journals.sagepub.com/author-instructions/REL

Welcomes submissions that provide a link between theory and practice

TESL Canada Journal

teslcanadajournal.ca/index.php/tesl/about/submissions

Publishes explanations of classroom activity, commentary on current topics, and reviews of teaching resources in English and in French

The TESL Electronic Journal

www.tesl-ej.org/wordpress

Invites submissions of articles and reviews of books, media resources, and websites

TESOL Connections

www.tesol.org/read-and-publish/newsletters-other-publications /tesol-connections/submit-features-or-resources-for-tesol-connections

An electronic newsletter that invites submissions of short articles (1,400 words) and quick classroom tips (500 words)

TESOL International Association Interest Section Newsletters

www.tesol.org/professional-development/publications-and-research /tesol-publications/

Join a TESOL International Association interest section and contact the newsletter editor for publication and editing opportunities

TESOL Journal

onlinelibrary.wiley.com/page/journal/19493533/homepage/ForAuthors.html

Publishes a variety of article types from full-length research articles to explorations of classroom perspectives

TESOL Resource Center

www.tesol.org/resource-center

TESOL International Association invites submissions of lesson plans, teaching tips, activities, and assessment instruments

References

Allwright, D. (1983). Classroom-centered research on language teaching and learning: A brief historical overview. *TESOL Quarterly, 17*(2), 191–204.

Allwright, D. (2005). From teaching points to learning opportunities and beyond. *TESOL Quarterly, 39*(1), 9–31.

Allwright, D., & Bailey, K.M. (1991). *Focus on the language classroom: An introduction to classroom research for language teachers.* Cambridge University Press.

Bailey, K. M., & Nunan, D. (Eds.). (1996). *Voices from the language classroom: Qualitative research on language education.* Cambridge University Press.

Borg, S. (2010). Language teacher research engagement. *Language Teaching, 43,* 391–429.

Borg. S. (2013). *Teacher research in language teaching: A critical analysis.* Cambridge University Press.

Brown, J. D., & Rodgers, T. S. (2002). *Doing second language research.* Oxford University Press.

Byrnes, H. (2016). Notes from the editor: Celebrating 100 years of *The Modern Language Journal. Modern Language Journal, 100*(Supplement 2016), 3–18.

Casanave, C., & Vandrick, S. (Eds.). (2003). *Writing for scholarly publication: Behind the scenes in language education.* Lawrence Erlbaum Associates.

Clarke, M. A. (1994). The dysfunctions of the theory/practice discourse. *TESOL Quarterly, 28*(1), 9–26.

Dawson, S. (2017). EAP learners explore their language learning lives through Exploratory Practice. In T. Stewart (Ed.), *TESOL voices: Insider accounts of classroom life—Higher Education* (pp. 7–13). TESOL Press.

Edge, J. (Ed.). (2001). *Action research.* TESOL Press.

Edge, J. (2002). *Continuing cooperative development: A discourse framework for individuals as colleagues.* University of Michigan Press.

Ellis, R. R. (2012). *Language teaching research and language pedagogy.* Wiley-Blackwell.

Farrell, T. S. C. (2006). (Ed.). *Language teacher research* (6 volume series). TESOL Press.

Freeman, D. (1996). Redefining the relationship between research and what teachers know. In K. M. Bailey & D. Nunan (Eds.), *Voices from the language classroom* (pp. 88–115). Cambridge University Press.

Freeman, D. (1998). *Doing teacher research*. Heinle & Heinle.

Hanks, J. (2017). *Exploratory practice in language teaching*. Palgrave Macmillan.

Hargittai, E. (2011, September 25). From review to publication. *Inside Higher Ed*. https://www.insidehighered.com/advice/2011/09/26/review-publication

Holliday, A. (2004). Issues of validity in progressive paradigms of qualitative research. *TESOL Quarterly, 38*(4), 731–734.

Kiely, R. (2014). Connecting with teachers: The case for language teaching research in the social sciences. *ELT Journal, 68*, 442–450.

Long, M. H. (1984). Process and product in ESL program evaluation. *TESOL Quarterly, 18*(3), 409–425.

MacKay, S. L. (2006). *Researching second language classrooms*. Lawrence Erlbaum Associates.

Maneekhao, K., & Todd, R. W. (2001). Two kinds of becoming: The researcher's tale and the mentor's tale. In J. Edge (Ed.), *Action research* (pp. 57–68). TESOL Press.

Marsden, E., & Kasprowicz, R. (2017). Foreign language educators' exposure to research: Reported experiences, exposure via citations, and a proposal for action. *The Modern Language Journal, 101*(4), 613–642. https://doi.org/10.1111/modl.12426

Montgomery, C., & Smith, L. C. (2015). Bridging the gap between researchers and practitioners. *Die Unterrichtspraxis/Teaching German, 48*, 100–113. https://doi.org/10.1111/tger.10183

Nunan, D., & Bailey, K. M. (2009). *Exploring second language classroom research: A comprehensive guide*. Heinle, Cengage Learning.

Quirke, P. (2001). Hearing voices: A robust and flexible framework for gathering and using student feedback. In J. Edge (Ed.), *Action research* (pp. 81–91). TESOL Press.

Sato, M., & Loewen, S. (2019). Do teachers care about research? The research-pedagogy dialogue. *ELT Journal, 73*(1), 1–10. https://doi.org/10.1093/elt/ccy048

Schecter, S. R. (1997). My professional transformation. In C. P. Casanave & S. R. Schecter (Eds.), *On becoming a language educator: Personal essays on professional development* (pp. 101–108). Lawrence Erlbaum Associates.

Shohamy, E. (2004). Reflections on research guidelines, categories, and responsibility. *TESOL Quarterly, 38*(4), 728–731. https://doi.org/10.2307/3588291

Stenhouse, L. (1975). *An introduction to curriculum research and development*. Heinemann.

Stewart, T. (2006a). Teacher-researcher collaboration or teachers' research? *TESOL Quarterly, 40*(2), 421–430.

Stewart, T. (2006b). Bridging the classroom perception gap: Comparing learners' and teachers' understandings of what is learned. In T. S. C. Farrell (Ed.), *Language teacher research in Asia* (pp. 141–155). TESOL Press.

Stewart, T. (Ed.). (2017). *TESOL voices* (six-book series). TESOL Press.

TESOL International Association. (2014). *Research agenda 2014*. https://www.tesol.org/media/z22pn2hw/2014_tesol-research-agenda.pdf

Werbner, L. (2004). A rebuff inspires reflection. *Essential Teacher, 1*(4), 42–44.

Wharton, S. (2008). Becoming a writer: Community membership and discursive literacy. In S. Garton & K. Richards (Eds.), *Professional encounters in TESOL: Discourses of teachers in teaching* (pp. 218–231). Palgrave Macmillan.

Widdowson, H. G. (1990). Discourses of inquiry and conditions of relevance. In J. Alatis (Ed.), *Georgetown University round table on languages and linguistics 1990* (pp. 37–48). Georgetown University Press.

Widdowson, H. G. (2003). *Defining issues in English language teaching*. Oxford University Press.

Zeichner, K. M., & Noffke, S. E. (2001). Practitioner research. In V. Richardson (Ed.), *Handbook of research on teaching* (4th ed., pp. 298–330). American Educational Research Association.

Sample Classroom Research Report

Dawson, S. (2017). EAP learners explore their language learning lives through exploratory practice. In T. Stewart (Ed.), *Higher education* (pp. 7–13). TESOL International Association.

Available from https://bookstore.tesol.org/stewart--tim-contributor-588720.php

Susan Dawson, in collaboration with learners Phappim Ihara and Kan Zhang

Background

There are many publications with examples of teacher research that novices can read. In this appendix, I will briefly describe a chapter published in a volume that I edited for TESOL Press. The TESOL Voices series consists of six books: *Preservice Teacher Education*; *Young Learner Education*; *Secondary Education*; *Adult Education*; *Higher Education*; and *Online and Hybrid Classroom Education*. This series showcases the voices of students and teachers as insider accounts of classroom life by participants in various TESOL environments. Susan Dawson's chapter explores a way to empower learners and include them as active participants in classroom research.

Exploratory Practice Defined

This chapter illustrates how the principles of exploratory practice (EP) can be put into practice. Allwright (2005) developed exploratory practice as a way for students and teachers "to develop their own understandings of life in the language classroom" (p. 361) while they are engaged in activities for learning and teaching. In other words, everyday pedagogic activities can become openings for greater understanding. Ideally, pedagogy and inquiry become inherently sustainable through EP. The focus of EP is on raising the quality of classroom life for teachers and students through greater understanding, not problem-solving, improvement, or efficiency. EP is organized around seven principles:

Principle 1: Put "quality of life" first.

Principle 2: Work primarily to understand language classroom life.

Principle 3: Involve everybody.

Principle 4: Work to bring people together.

Principle 5: Work for mutual development.

Principle 6: Integrate the work for understanding into classroom practice.

Principle 7: Make the work a continuous enterprise.

(Allwright, 2003, pp. 128–130)

Learners are positioned as co-investigators as they strive to become the best learners that they can be. Students are encouraged to find puzzling aspects of the language classroom to investigate as part of their regular study. The seven principles build on Dewey's (1933) inquiry-based approach to education and Freire's (2006) critical pedagogy.

Description of Context

Susan's English for Academic Purposes class at a private language school in England met 20 hours a week. It was a class for international students hoping to progress to a master's degree course at a British university. The objective of Susan's class was to introduce academic and research skills to the 16 students, including writing, time management, and reflective skills.

Finding a Focus

By using EP in her class, Susan had students set their own agenda for learning, allowing them to explore something they felt was important for them while directing the EP work to help fulfill the course objectives. Two to three hours per week were dedicated to the EP work for greater understanding. Susan first gave an introductory lecture on EP and asked the class, "What puzzles you about your language learning lives?" Next, she gave students time to think about puzzling aspects of their language learning and to write the puzzles out. This exercise generated 40 puzzles. Later, students chose the puzzle they were most interested in to investigate and formed groups with others who wanted to explore the same puzzle. The puzzles (unedited) students chose were:

- Why do I have so few ideas during IELTS speaking test?
- Why do I always speak English in wrong grammar although I know how to use grammar?
- Why can't I pay more attention in listening task?
- Why do I feel nervous and make mistakes when I chat with foreigners?
- Why does team 3 (near the door) always speak in Chinese?

Susan helped her students focus these puzzles into researchable questions. Then, over several weeks, students thought about how to investigate the questions and collect and analyse data. After making those determinations, they wrote individual reports and presented their findings to students and teachers in other classes. Susan integrated much of the language study of the course into the written report and group presentations.

Group Investigations

Susan asked two of her students to write up brief descriptions of their group EP investigations. Phappim's group chose to investigate the following puzzle: Why do I always speak English in wrong grammar although I know how to use grammar? After discussing this question for some time, the group decided to explore it through a questionnaire for other students and teachers. They discovered that many people felt the same way. Most people commented that it was important to keep trying and not worry too much about making mistakes. They expressed frustration at not finding a single solution to their dilemma, but said they better understood the importance of speaking with confidence.

Kan's group decided to focus on the following puzzle: Why does team 3 (near the door) always speak in Chinese? The group investigated this puzzle primarily through observation. They observed the interactions of other groups in the class once an hour for 5 minutes. During their observations, they noted the number of people who spoke in Chinese, for how long, and what they spoke about. They also interviewed other classmates to find out the reasons people spoke their native language during lessons. The students discovered that they were not trying to speak English as much as they probably should. They recommended that the administration and teachers become stricter about using English in class. They found that the engagement with EP was good preparation for the International English Language Testing System (IELTS) Writing Task 1. In addition, by repeating their presentation several times during the poster carousel, they gained confidence to speak without notes.

Teacher Perspective

Susan's research question was to learn more about how to integrate EP principles into her teaching. She has another longstanding puzzle, which is: Why is the pull of solutions so attractive to learners? EP is aimed at deepening understanding, but Susan found that her students were focused on achieving the required score on the IELTS. She honestly reflects that it might not be realistic to expect students in a high-stakes English for Academic Purposes course to be comfortable with the ambiguity that EP investigations often generate. In the final analysis, it seems that Susan's efforts did spark the beginning of a culture of inquiry in the class. In follow-up interviews a few months after the course ended, "many learners said how useful the EP work had been in helping them develop a more critical, confident, and inquiring approach to their studies" (Dawson, 2017, p. 12).

Susan Dawson has been incorporating the inclusive practitioner research framework of EP into her teaching for many years. EP is one way that some teachers have used to combine course work while simultaneously attempting to gain a deeper learning about their own puzzles and those of their students.

References

Allwright, D. (2003). Exploratory practice: Rethinking practitioner research in language teaching. *Language Teaching Research, 7*(2), 113–141. https://doi.org/10.1191/1362168803lr118oa

Allwright, D. (2005). Developing practitioner principles for the case of exploratory practice. *The Modern Language Journal, 89*(3), 353–366. https://doi.org/10.1111/j.1540-4781.2005.00310.x

Dewey, J. (1933). *How we think: A restatement of the relation of reflective thinking to the educative process.* D.C Heath and Company.

Freire, P. (2006). *Pedagogy of the oppressed.* Continuum.

About the Author

Tim Stewart has worked as a TESOL educator since 1986. When he entered the field, he was fortunate to have had wonderful colleagues who opened their classrooms and collaborated with him while team teaching. This early foundation set Tim off on a career in TESOL that centred on professional discovery through classroom research. Tim's quest to learn more about his students and his teaching practice led him to publish more than 50 articles and book chapters while authoring or editing 13 books. His early experiences teaching showed him that the classroom is a fascinating crucible of learning, and he quickly appreciated that teachers need to tell the stories that emerge from their classrooms. Tim has tried to pass this message on to other TESOL classroom teachers and graduate students over the years. He will always value the learning he has gained through his classroom practice and research as he prepares to retire from Kyoto University and move on to do other things.

About the Series Editor

Thomas S. C. Farrell, PhD, is a professor at Brock University, Canada. His professional interests include reflective practice and second language teacher education and development. He has published widely in these areas. His work can be found at www.reflectiveinquiry.ca.